Real Karaoke People

Real Karaoke People

poems and prose by Ed Bok Lee

To Justin,

Brother Soul
in this Living Story
of Words...

The sky Plows Home!

Peace & Bless,

E[signature]

Berkeley, CA
1/28/06

n e W
Many Voices
Project Winner

© 2005 by Ed-Bok Lee
First Edition
Library of Congress Control Number: 2005923890
ISBN: 0-89823-226-0
Cover design and interior book design by Katie Elenberger
Cover photography by Bob Wimmer
Author photograph by Charissa Uemura

The publication of *Real Karaoke People* is made possible by the generous support of the Jerome Foundation and other contributors to New Rivers Press. Additional support is provided by The McKnight Foundation.

For academic permission please contact Frederick T. Courtright at 570-839-7477 or permdude@ eclipse.net. For all other permissions, contact The Copyright Clearance Center at 978-750-8400 or info@copyright.com.

New Rivers Press is a nonprofit literary press associated with Minnesota State University Moorhead.

Wayne Gudmundson, Director
Alan Davis, Senior Editor
Thom Tammaro, Poetry Editor
Donna Carlson, Managing Editor
    Honors Apprentice: Rosanne Pfenning
    Real Karaoke People book team: Jens Larson, Heather Steinmann
Editorial interns: Fauntel DeShayes, Tessa Dietz, Kacy Friddle, Diana Goble, Jill Haugen,
    Amber Langford, Jens Larson, Samantha Miller, Kurt Olerud, Tamera Parrish,
    Heather Steinmann, Melissa Sumas, Abbey Thompsen,
Design interns: Katie Elenberger, Allison Garske, Amanda Ketterling,
    Jocie Salveson, Lindsay Staber, Amy Wilcox.
Communications Coordinator: Gerri Stowman; Teresa Schafer
Literary Festival Coordinator: Jill Haugen
    Fundraising Coordinator: Jens Larson
    Web Site Coordinator: Conor Shenk
Marlane Sanderson; Deb Hval: Business Manager
Allen Sheets: Design Manager
Nancy Hanson: Events Manager
Liz Conmey: Marketing Manager

Printed in the United States of America.

Many Voices Project Number 107

New Rivers Press
c/o MSUM
1104 7th Avenue South
Moorhead, MN 56563
www.newriverspress.com

For my family

All love is immigrant.

Every year a ghost
needing more

to let go.

contents

I.

at mihwangsa temple

Nothing today but a girl
who flaps the wooden rafters
calligraphied on a silk-white ribbon.

A red candle some cold fingers lit
to memorialize her early death.

Bronze bowl of fresh figs
and black flies. Fertility
unnerved.

Someone remind the wind
everything is already swept away
in the afterlife.

And wonder
like a flame's grace
should possess no weight.

Who she was.
What anyone does to slip
through evening's mask of trees.

A strange lust, this life.
Everywhere beautiful souls
bathing in grief.

sokcho in butterfly dust

Beside my father's window hung a portrait
of Sokcho—a seaside village where lather laps
the morning shore like cold rice porridge.
A watercolor adorned with butterfly pluckings: tiny
fishermen on docks pulling rods of antennae,
silk lines cast beneath a flaming dusk
of fanned harlequin wings.

I'd imagine the blithe figures
whistling to work in the fall.
Sadly-happy Korean faces, hung over
from soju, smoked squid, and cards till dawn.
Sometimes I'd enter the shadowy port;
rock asleep inside any one of the turquoise junks
as the moon's mothy swoosh brightened a path
back across the ocean.

Life should always be this easy to find.
A small boy waiting for his father to return for dinner.

Meanwhile, esoteric seafarers travel
back and forth between one rough, one finer world,
on land, over sea and the coral
trove we learn to navigate
by drowning.

inside lake heron

Summertime, splash it
with Pabst Blue Ribbon
beer to bitter the smoke
over sizzling strips of paper-thin

soy sauce and sugar-marinated beef
our mothers grill, stifling
laughter with hands like schoolgirls.
Follies gossiped about others less

or too much like them.
Blowing at gnats and flies,
chopping garlic on a flat stone,
sweet pregnant watermelon, sucking

teeth and hissing tongues.
As the men row across the lake's
summer yawn, baiting time till Monday;
noisy hours at the sugar beet plant,

auto shop, grocery, liquor and
health food store, office or
if fluent enough with English,
a service desk, maybe even a blackboard.

Trolling for the Lord's deep shifting will,
one stung aqueous muscle hoisted at a time;
pinching fingers through black eyes to calm
and unhook the thrashing lives...

I remember Mr. Choi, who drove a nail
with his forehead through a two-by-four
every winter to enroll young and old
tae kwon do hopefuls at the Civic Auditorium,

teetering in an aluminum boat mid-lake;
crooning into a microphone bottle of beer
of some blue evening side street in Seoul.
A primal cry so small and wide across the waves,

to our shorebound ears it was the voice
of Jesus standing on water, faltering
in faith, desperate to hit
the right note with smoky lungs, struggling

to not drown in this land
with four other drunk Koreans.
The men in a boat.
The women around a fire.

And we, their sun-burnt sons and daughters,
chasing minnows and perch
from the dock with spinning daredevils
and one aluminum net, swung

like some blind angel's stunted appendage.
Never straying far from the stories
any mother weaves into dreams
with the water in her voice...

Sometimes we'd fall completely in
and ask: What happened?

Spell-broken, they'd laugh.
No, really, what happened to pretty Mrs. Han

who tattooed too much black liner
to the rims of each eye to become
a raccoon grocery shopping
only after midnight? Did she

die? Or the Lim first son who won
a full ride to Princeton, then got expelled
for stabbing some blue blood in a dining club?
Tell us, please, what happened to the old waitress from Pusan

who left her nineteen-year-old GI husband from Wisconsin
for an Ethiopian carpet saleswoman in Bloomington,
never heard from again? What *about* those
two young lovers during the war, who leapt

from the roof of a Buddhist temple?
Or were those all just songs
that summer the men shared Marlboros
on a pontoon; hawked and swore, spat and hummed

along to shinawi on a portable eight-track player?
While the women on shore later ignored
the drunk, deepening slurs; macho
twistings of an apple into crisp halves,

my father, with the larger hands of a man
bred during war, smiling now, offering

one to every child. Later at night
bolting up, screaming of his leg lit by Communists

in a coffin beneath the floorboards.
Or sometimes not sleeping at all.
Guns re-polished in the cabinet,
slapping his children's faces for talking back;

smacks against whoever tries to protect them.
So much that never adds up.
Seven thousand dollars and a back-breaking month
spent to renovate a moldy church no one wanted

at first. Divided by Amway and Coleco
investments withdrawn from his children's college fund.
They tanked. Minus the vegetable garden,
where father, son, and daughter

fertilize the earth with fish guts
because the Lord created us
to feed other living things
whatever we possess.

Added to the weight of a rake pressed to my throat
for not using it right. Multiplied by
the pages of poetry by Kim Sowol,
whose words even now

echo blackbird wings shadowing
across Yongbyun Mountain. Men

of that generation were born in flames,
so the women learned to love through water

and somehow forgive those moments
when the sky suddenly changed
and everything smoldered gray.
But what about their children;

the stories they became?
Translations for what
my father meant while dying
in the hospital he kept reminding

me to check every month
the tire pressure and oil
in my mother's car?
Who will accompany those

moments of sunset
when the men row home,
the children grow the fire
and the women begin to dance

so deep and slow
the whole afternoon
is submerged?

la vida loca —*for Mat Yang*

Sister skins the mango
with a spoon and says
it's the color of a cheek
that's been kissed
or has kissed
she won't share.

Mother is weeping in her private chamber
in the Castle, watching drama-videos
from the old country, her callused feet
propped next to a plate of rice and porkchop scraps.

"Revolution makes even a queen do things she never expected,
High Commissioner."

Father, a ghost of smoke and sweat in the kitchen,
swims these days through the classifieds
in search of employment, used auto parts, cheap
dream real estate; his international
radio out of tune.

"Livin' La Vida Loca!"

Just another summer in South Minneapolis,
so humid my homies miss handhugs
between slick layups, swooshing
chainmetal at will till the sun sinks
the last three pointer from way out …

or that Jovina Sharms
in dark sunglasses and no bra underneath

everyone's sheer red imagination struts past,
parting pushers and thugs in front of Super America
like some girl-child Moses.

Shit, who needs that.
When I got my silver Pinto flying
faster than the white stripes I hand-painted on the spoiler
will allow, on my way
with a pocketful of change
to the New Asia Market for a can
of Young Coconut Juice.

frozen in the sky

It's so cold I'm dying, says the old man.
His walking cane knobbed in one cracked hand,
the other comforting a Good News Bible.

We stand in line at the Sunrise Doughnut Shop,
this mumbling U.S. Army veteran
and I. Dark-skinned, unshaven gray for days;

his one good eye black as onyx
polished to perfect. This winter
he's wrapped himself in a blue plastic tarp

pinned with a Purple Heart. This old
Indian, Puerto Rican, Mulatto, Mestizo,
whatever he is to me, I don't know. He smells

like the story of my grandfather, who survived two wars
but couldn't stop talking
of the sour urine that plagued the refugee camps

no matter how many times you washed
your belongings in the rain. You know the smell,
that evil homeless stench

alive in a flattened length of cardboard
left on the street, impressed with the paler shape
of a soul whose body's been long

cleared away by the wind and leaves.
I saved your people, says the old man.
A toothless wad of day-old sugartwist

on his tongue. Curdled body
of the second coming, or muffled
lament of a dozen gook legs and bellies

choking the rice paddies
in Saigon. No Gun Ri.
Iwo Jima. Bataan.

Bullet against bone ash,
butane flame to gangrene,
tank tracks on the back scarring mountains...

When my mother describes the corpse
of her baby brother, slung to the crooked spine
of their grandmother, she has no tears.

They are long frozen on the road down to Seoul
she and millions more walked
when the Communists declared victory in the North.

1945. The icy earth was too hard to bury
the little boy's dehydrated shape. It was so cold
I couldn't feel a thing, my mother explains with amazement.

Sometimes the soldiers would throw us
matches from their jeeps. Once Haesuni
got a Hershey bar for just talking

to a young GI. And then the Soviet air bombers arrived.
One blonde soldier wrapped in a head bandage
rifled us into a pigpen.

Don't move! he screamed. Who are you!
Both eyes landmine craters. Gone.
So we ran, all five of us, your aunt fell down;

I tried to carry her, seven years old, mid-winter,
but it was so cold, my hands were stone, my bare feet
like wooden pegs, and I was on stilts

balancing a mile above that frozen road
toward a gray horizon. At night I thought
I might turn into a dying bird

and fall asleep in the wind, drifting
high above the choppy ocean.
Because birds, you know, the noble ones at least,

before they die, they fly out over a great body of water.
Greater than their own visions can see across.
They keep flapping and hurling

their bodies at the wind
until they can't move their ancient wings anymore;
until they've journeyed so far

pure exhaustion finally frees
their battered destinies
over to the breeze

and waves
and traffic
on Franklin Avenue

yesterday, when I saw that old man on the street corner.
His white breath obscuring whether he was speaking truth
or just amusing himself.

Some intoxicated archangel
explaining the ways of the world to passing cars,
or just another casualty

of a forgotten war.
A living monument, or blundered memory.
A muttering prophecy

or echo from the past
coming straight for me.
Whether he also sees

dead frozen soldiers,
women
and children

chewing ice,
shrapnel,
feathers

and kidneys on the road to heaven
in his dreams…
Or just another face

on the sidewalk staring
into the paper cup
he jangles to be free.

a fable of fruit

remember that old Japanese-American grocer in Anaheim,
stump-legged and propped before his till

how he lobbed you a dusty tomato
and your sister asked: what happened to him

your mother called to her,
while he whispered in your ear
he was a secret agent in the war,
and probably, someday
you would get drafted too,
and then what would you do,
who will you serve, which people
will you kill

                and what will *you* lose

                        +

they will teach you many things in school
about Negroes, coolies, obedient Indian wives of Europeans

the names will change, but the expressions stay the same:
progress through annihilation of spiritual difference

until forgetfulness slowly sets in
like Eurydice unfurling
her golden arms too far and plunging
into the heart of the Mississippi from a raft
to grasp the moon like Li Po,
or was it Clint Eastwood,
or some other
outlaw

no, it was only your grandfather,
old Confucian reciter of poems, now lost
in his final years; wandering
home from his pigeons in the park

the terror on his face when you found him
seated under an elm, long past dinnertime,
unable to speak your name, the *Book of Changes*
in one hand, the other
aiming a TV remote at the sky

+

Midwestern wood, scrap metal and marrow;
if you walk to Cedar and Lake,
past Bituminous Roadways, you see
the rotting tooth-like tombs of the Pioneer Cemetery
from the Indian Wars, Spanish-American War:
how the country began

some nights you hear
wind strumming the wrought-iron gates,
a high-low wail flagged by old news and beer bottles

are the dead horse-men souls
happy or sad

did the Korean War save my father's life
or divide it

now there's talk of attacks, bravery and loyalty again

but where does America end
and the story of barbed wire begin

tonight they're flashlighting foreign faces in cars:
Muslims, South Asians, dark features and eyes;
airing sweat-lit mugshots on CNN,
your freedom or your life,
detained indefinitely in fluorescent prison cells
without charge

meanwhile shipping to a desert across the sea other friends in
     fatigues:
human coal to brighten the night's search for peace

✦

once, an old Nisei tossed me an heirloom tomato
and insisted it was neither fruit nor vegetable, but something else

I bit into the flat, eerie face
that stared back

our hair

Who disturbed whose dream
unable to sleep the midnight we drove
downtown for a film? It turned out
not the *Rocky Horror Picture Show*
but a porno. In that moldy
church of a crumbling theater
with five lonely others, one old man
coughed over his body's work;
another confessed to the liquid-lit screen. `

You slipped your icy hand down
my pants recounting all the kisses
you never saw your Vietnamese parents exchange;
never heard I love yous or sorrys
sweeten or mend
the heavy air
they brought to this land.

Instead you witnessed
red peppers, squash, snap peas
each season in plastic pails lining the steps
and counters. Shaded labor
from a garden they nourished
side by side
their whole lives buried
in soil rich as our hair;
deeper than the hunger
of children, birds, invisible
seeds warm and tender
as tongues in prayer.

year of the dog

hot in the year of the dog, i sip whiskey and coke on my roof-
top; sparrows weaving together this summer evening full of
nothing but two shirtless Mexicans, my neighbors, mustached
Elvises in the twilight, who once took a chicken apart with
gloves of blood and feathers, and now pickax a gravel echo
deep in the back alley of this immigrant tale leading to dust and
broken bottles

one of them, wiping away the sun's last rays
from his forehead, looks up and stares at the heart within the
cough of his sweaty son, or brother, cousin, fellow man

they
come, i know, for their children, these two Ezekiels of daily-
dishwashed hands and fry-pocked countenance; come
for their women, raven-maned Marias hanging damp tube
socks, stained workshirts, and pajama tops from branches
and chain link; come like anyone to this neighborhood in
Minneapolis, from Mexico, Sudan, the hills of Laos and Tien
Shen Mountains, packed at the backs of night banana trucks,
faceless, alienesque ghosts in border patrol heat-sensing
photos, stuffed in shrimp trawlers and gassy trunks of cars,
each day negotiating a border of stars, hauling summer nights
and salty dreams, lit by Bics and stooped by the moon on their
backs. come because God intoned they'd otherwise end up
like him, on a fishhook in the sea

only to arrive late every night
like my mother, who places her cast-iron rice cooker of twenty
years on the curb. through the window i watch not her stoop
and limp, but the dilapidated slippers which carry her to this far

end of the world; helpless slippers i once hid, but long to eat
now from the dumpster of my dreams

                                visions, incantations
so slippery tonight, in hands clinking dishes, turning bolts;
listen closely how they chop, slice, zip, sew, push, pull, tug,
bend, but never ever break; see their swollen factory feet years
underneath eyes bleary on Sunday evenings at the Target
on Lake Street, four minutes before closing, an entire Somali
family parts the doors like a sea of glass, Mother cloaked in
blue tunic and hijab, Father in flip-flops, five young children
inside; the smallest of them stops and stares back at me
through Mohammedan angel eyes, holding a potted cactus
and Koran, as if challenging me to remember his fate. is he our
hero at age seven, or the villain?

                              come for your job, your home,
your daughter's blonde uterus, your son's black soul; the
Laundromat your family built up and protected with bullets of
sweat, only to watch it torn down by similar fingers clutching
torches and shopping carts loaded down with beef and stereo
equipment, L.A. Riots '92!, like locusts come, killer bees, gypsy
moths you can't see stealing fruit in their infinitesimal hands,
tax dollars, unemployment; come to ESL classes, stretching
verbs and adjectives to place their plucked tongues back on
mango trees, chestnut, rambutan; stumbling through burning
jungle brush and a heaven of metal detectors, skipping over a
dozen words for water, scales of scars from paramilitary raids
in the dark, tattoos sun- and wind-carved like mishealed wing
joints, fleeing fourteen-year-old soldiers wielding hacksaws
across scorched savanna,

only to end up in Fargo, Rochester,
Wabasha, Wisconsin, humming along to the pitch and fall of
a snowy drift alone in a borrowed bedroom; refugees from
Bosnia and Saigon, come to till the abandoned prairies, ghost
towns of a century-and-a-half ago, where Swedish songs of
sugar beet farmers mist the one-room church houses

if you
concentrate, you can still hear their wails in the wind; journey
the spine of abandoned railroads on the Dakota Plains to
the end of civilization, past vagrant, shot-through Indian
reservations, and you know how they came, but where did
they go?

these guardians of the night's floating soul; these
aching knees, palms and fingernails hauling ten generations of
shadow and soil,

this family living next door in the twilight

who used to be my own.

the hole

That July we smashed pennies
with a ball-peen hammer into quarter-
sized slugs and ransacked

every pop machine we could find.
The silver boon transformed in the coin return
was not power, but freedom. To take

taxis to movies, arcades, even once
proposition a hooker on Broadway.
She smirked, but stopped

long enough to ask how much we had.
I was nine, maybe ten.
I'd seen prettier carnival ride operators.

Whadyouwant? she asked.
Her eyeballs right through us.
So we gave her eighteen dollars to show

her hole. In a back alley
crunching broken glass, she unbuckled
her metal skull belt, coughing

and bent over. Life and Death
inside that moment like a giant
shadow longing to stab itself.

And then they caught us.
At the VA hospital, a week later,
in the sub-basement.

An old man in a robe wandering the halls
with a purple surgical cage markered on his face,
pointed us out by the Pepsi machine

to a nurse and two cops.
We could have flung our change. Fled
up the stairwell or around that corridor

where they gurneyed the dead.
But we knew the summer
had already closed

its humid legs heavy with debt
around everything we could
ever hope to possess.

hungry butterflies

That gave you more confidence:
To absorb the Mini-Mart incandescence before
gliding a Snickers or Combos down your pants
then walk out like you didn't exist.

Sometimes Hsu slipped a whole box
of M&Ms or a case of Mountain Dew
into the bathroom, climbed the toilet and stretching on
tippy toes to a ceiling panel,
stashed the booty for any gut later.

Then perfumed sex cracked its gum at us.
Softer hands that let us guide them for just
a few kisses
or tears, hidden
underneath layers of wonder
like a steel butterfly knife
twirling afterward.

dizzier days

Other days we'd faint.
Deep breaths and palms
clamped to carotid artery
till you woke on your back, swarmed
by crimson pinpoints flashing
signals you fucked death in the face.
Or we'd pulverize our parents' sleeping
or diet tablets into lines; play video games
till no slap could flinch more than your eyelids.
When we lost interest in ditchweed,
Rush, whippets, Liquid Paper, blackberry brandy
older than the thirteen-year blood inside us,
we turned to girls. What's the lure
of a baby sitter? The illusion
of ownership...illegitimate parentage?
Once my girlfriend locked twins
in the basement with an Atari machine
and joined four of us on a new waterbed
wearing only a full body leotard.
You can vandalize anything
for free. Streetlights, urinals,
church windows, fences,
entire bean fields. Another rainy afternoon
seven of us smashed a kid's heart
up against the wall of his trailer home
till he passed out and convulsed on the linoleum.
A velvet Jesus offered robed arms behind us.
One night we stole a car and launched it into a lake.
But we never did dig anything up
from that graveyard by the river
meant for those who had no name

or family to claim their stink.
Balding grass on dirt clumped
hard like walking on fists. We were
American boys who could guzzle Shasta,
frozen pizza rolls, pickles
and white bread any hour we wanted.
Three of us now dead.
Two buried on a hill.
The third no one knows.
His mom, a biker barmaid,
rode his ashes out of state.
His younger sister's a mess now.
I see her around one street corner
picking her lips and cheeks as if
larvaed with rot. Once I bought her
lasagna and recounted the story of the Pontiac
we dumped. How her brother
believed something valuable
lay locked inside the glove compartment.
We tried to mock him into giving up.
He just kicked us out and gunned it
toward the dock. We all laughed,
and walked home that night high
on something as the stars
vomited their music.
Some people go forever like this.
Searching for a stronger heart
in Jesus or some other
luminescent abyss. Alive
to friends and family,
but anonymously dead.

ars poeticana

today a poem should be read while watching a trashy talk show.
while everyone is howling over each other. a thin, resonant
voice seeping through all the hard drop sex pot flesh shots and
howls. a poem should be painted on a runway, heaven split in
two overhead by the roar of a DC-10, so close it takes the part
out of your mind

a poem should talk about gods, race, flowers and class as if
they possessed equal mass, all
in the voice of an ancient Greek or Tibetan statue; a whirling
dervish with one alabaster wing, the other an obsidian palm
offering a crystal shard of the Tao

a poem should infiltrate
labor union meetings to float the tie-breaking vote to strike with
the weight of the single slip of paper it's written upon,
a single word: yes or no

once read out loud a poem should swallow itself
to remember a universe
inside a larger universe inside an even larger darkness
cold as the open mouth of a dead Chechen
grandmother on a gravel road;
the bus driver steps out, feels the body with his boot, hauls her
to the side, and drives on

a poem would have done something,
not just sat studying genitive case endings;
at least placed something of itself underneath
the woman's head amid the marsh's mosquitoey music

a poem is the only antidote to regret;
a perfume whose essence is the glorious armpit
of a hungry people in the projects or suburbs;
a New York City penthouse where bread and roses ordered up
from the blue streets below
will never be enough

some people know
how to listen for subtle notes in the rain
bleating cars and concrete, mailbox heads, empty of
correspondence;
b-sharp against a storm drain roaring back to the sea

a poem is sound mouthing sense,
the spitty fluorescence i'm trying to sign to you with my tongue
under hot lights, my face already a blur, my body cinders wind-
blown to both sides of the equator, my words a flock of blue
birds soaring over the gaping grave of my mouth in the earth i've
escaped for as long as i can believe all poems are full of fuchsia
veins and spiral spears of grass,
bindi dots and ancient cans of Old Milwaukee,
telephones in the Parthenon, aphid sweat,
any hieroglyph for 'aphrodisiac'

everything indestructible
that can't be photographed

once, when knives were musical instruments,
and garlic made people generous,
and every man and woman was yoked by stars,
every child able to resuscitate the future,

poetry wasn't poetry

it was just another way
to gossip about stones reproducing
without having to brag of one's heart

kimchi

A stone from my mother's garden sits by the sink,
solitary as the sunlight
she rinsed it in.

Two pounds to hold down
napa cabbage, garlic and red pepper
in brine. A humid eight-day foment
stuffed into gallon-sized glass. Sprinkles
of ground anchovies to nourish the spirit
tiny-gurgling up like a lunged life
through the kimchi's orange blood.

+

This pungent dish a peasant
on M*A*S*H once presented the army doctors
for retrieving his squinty life from certain death.

I awaited Klinger's and Hawkeye's expressions
as they undid the mysterious clay pot
I knew to them would smell like garbage.
The laugh track poised…

Then my father entered and switched the television off.

the secret to life in america

My brother sits me down and tells me
the secret to life in America.
I'm twelve years old when this happens.
He grabs my shoulders and says:
No one likes an immigrant.
It reminds them of when they fell down
and no one was around to help them.
When they couldn't talk.
As children when they got lost in public.
Cold and wet, everyone hates an immigrant.

So don't trust nobody.
The Whites, they'll teach you
to hate yourself for being silent.
They'll punish you for fighting back.
They'll love the taste of your food and culture, and sister…
and yet spit you out.

The Blacks, at first you'd think they understand loss.
But to them you're just another cracker with a bad case of
    jaundice.
Don't expect shit from them,
they can't afford to be generous.
Latins laugh at you behind your back.
Do you know this? I'm trying to tell you
how it is in the city,
he says.

I ask my brother if I can go outside now.

No! he screams. Our father is dead
and now I have to teach you
how to survive
in America.

Fags are everywhere.
And they want you. 'Cause
to them you're exotic and cute
and will do all the dirty work.
The Chinese look down on you
for using their alphabet. The Japanese have raped
your women through the centuries
and will do it again. In fact, never
do business with other Asians,
'cause they're the greediest people alive.
Next to Jews.

Now I'm crying, because my brother
has pulled off his work shirt.

Open your eyes!
This is where that black boy pulled the trigger
over twenty dollars and a candy bar! Here
is where the Whites punctured my kidney in a parking lot
        outside of Denny's…
And the Mexicans just kept drinking their beers.
This is the bruise on my soul
where every American girl ever looked at me
like I was still the enemy.
This is where Agent Orange first set in.
This is where the DMZ line is still drawn!

Taste the barbed wire on my tongue!
See where that fat white teacher called me a freak
for getting a B in math! Feel
my broken immigrant's throat
that couldn't tell him to Fuck Off!!!
    These are my yellow hands!
This is my cock!
These are my eyes wide open!
This is my heart filled with cigarette smoke!
This my aching back
which brought you here
and buried our father!
    This is the cheek mother slapped
for the way that I called her
ignorant.

    This is the *GQ* subscription sister gave me for
    Christmas.

Here is my blood, which tastes just like tears.
These are my dreams for the future
dead and shriveled in the corner.
This is my broom. This the face
I couldn't save from myself.
Are you listening to any of this?

    Yes, I tell him. I'm listening.

You're lucky, he says. You'll go to college
when you grow up.

I don't know, I tell him.

Work your ass off and move away from this shit hole
out to the suburbs. Maybe marry
a white girl.

I don't know, I tell him.

Go off and write... Poetry.

I won't, I say.

Yes you will. And when you do,
do me this one favor.

What, I ask.

Lie.
And make our father and me

the heroes

you always needed us to be.

that smell

ey, what is that smell

skulking through the city this summer,
snapping at my dreams like a headless
duck on hooks, 24-hour fish guts
at an open-air market in Mokpo;

pink light, old tripe, sour milk and cilantro
brightening my pho broth; night fluorescent-lit jar
of snake blood, soft serpent curl
fetal in formaldehyde like the live bait

we used to watch old fishermen catch octopus
with in crab pots; a ripening rice paddy
and roasted silkworms sold in newspaper cones
on the steam-cold streets of Seoul;

what waters my mouth and fills my heart...
emboldening the dab of sesame oil
my uncle slicked into his hair in Pagoda Park
to get all the girls; a Hyundai motor scooter sputtering by

a vomit-bombed sidewalk in the blue after-club hour of dawn;
old jar of tiger balm and rice cooker steaming up
all my windows this fall; mushy persimmon
whose skin slips right off the meat;

orange strings we loved to pull and pluck
from our teeth like musical instruments; barley tea
sipped with honey and songs Emo learned

in a Texas sweatshop full of sewing machines

and three dozen other sleepy-eyed immigrant
wives of GIs, garlic-munching Godzillas;
go on chew two packs of Doublemint, but still look out!
cuz that smell gets into your skin, ghost-inhabits

your pores and ceilings, grease-stains the brain
sniffffffffffffff   early August, you *know*
what that smell is strutting down Canal…
Chinatown! where a glazed pig's head presides over

its butcherman, waiter, dishwasher; the waft
of undocumented, south-of-the-border sweat
that wipes down all the kitchens I ever worked in;
a firetruck racing to purge this red chili pepper of a tongue;

that smell is the deer antler my grandmother
sawed and boiled to force-feed my anemic sister
with a teaspoon; impact of aluminum bat
that burst my brother's nose; milky rice

makkoli on me and my boys' intoxicated breaths
when we sing karaoke all night in K-town!
hurling broken battle cries like Chinese
gunpowder on the Fourth of July;

fresh horse meat, blowfish, rusty can
of betelnut juice, kumys, cold seaweed soup
and thousand-year-old egg…
what reeks the basement of our home,

not mold, but the handful of dust
my father carried to this land in his pocket:
a thousand and one white doves he later released
from the Golden Gate Bridge…

meanwhile my mother kneels on the kitchen floor,
hand-packing a jar of kimchi for the New Year;
in a weird reversal of my birth, she pulls
a fully formed ginseng root from the earth!

hands I watch a decade later, webbed with bleach and starch;
checking a pot over the lowest blue diamond of a flame
for me to consume alone after studying math and astronomy.
this fishhead soup still flows through my veins;

powered by a fleet of angels picking away
at equations and galaxies I applied to connect the crooked banks
of my littered spine and the Yellow Sea inside
only to find two cups love, four tablespoons war,

one teaspoon Japanese soldier pissing
in yet another Korean village well…
what a brown child standing naked in the rain
must taste like to God;

people shucking sugarcane
as they have for five thousand years, fermenting
beancurd, sour mutton and salted plantain
and it won't go away, cuz I'm here to tell you

that smell colors the Third World!

and if you can't take it, get off the planet,
cuz that shit is fish eyes and cheek meat that melts
on your tongue, sucking you way down,

a transatlantic monsoon; red curry, pepper, anise;
perfume of pure religion spinning
in a bowl of lotus blossom soup; cold cup
of chrysanthemum tea I once forgot

underneath my bed for a whole week,
chipped and blessed with a thousand kisses,
it flavored my dreams;
human musk

of my love's hair
sunk deep into her pillow;
all that is beautiful
spiritual, filling

cathedrals with the question:
who are we?
more sea or stone?
more journey or home?

sublime, elemental, old
mugwort, fried gosari,
desiccated mushrooms bagged
like the faces of grannies in plastic

hanbok dresses... what confuses

hunger for shame; the hidden
forest in my grandfather's beard,
clogged with spice and tea leaves, howling

stories of swords and demons…
a timeless knowing
it's about to rain
three days before…

the different scent between melted
snow and rainwater… animal,
universal; it is sex and death
and sunshine in one tiny bottle,

so drink it down all of it now while you can,
cuz that smell is the only thing
that led Buddha through the mountain!
it is not enclosed, but a wild open road;

not superficial, it cuts to the bone;
part fire, water, air and soil;
not canned flowers
or the suburbs,

but a monk winged with flames for his principles;
napalm, Agent Orange and severed tongues;
cash money smudged with blood, oil,
smart bombs, nerve gas and radioactive pus...

incense of prayer on my father's fingers

when he'd light the candles every Christmas Eve…
a strange koan I hold at the back of my throat,
ancient and fresh still as cherry blossoms each spring

in the song of the king's palace my mother hums
when she thinks nobody is listening…
floating fragrance I'm useless to hold
in the form of my grown sister

as she spoons pearly porridge
through my grandmother's lips
one moment at a time… all that is
strong, sweet and old

and everything else
heaped in the living garbage of my memory…

what feeds your soul?

water

Sertsa, this winter
snowflakes keep hypnotizing
submission, one unique
lash at a time.

The housefly somehow born
in my frosted window sees
Antarctica with its heart;

it is a song not for humans,
as any map of emotion so brief and intense
loses itself.

The clouds pass overhead
washing their white gloves.

I use the last of your red thread
as a divining rod.

skip ching porn king

My name is Skip Ching and I'm what you might call a porn king. You may have seen my latest video—*Skip Ching's Gang Bang Rides Again*, recently remastered on DVD. In it, I play an Oriental railroad worker turned cowhand, named...

...Skip Ching.

Since retiring from the profession, I've made it my personal mission in life to take to the road and talk openly about certain stereotypes folks seem to have about the porn industry. I am thus very happy to be standing here in front of you tonight at...

...Little Brothers and Friends of the Elderly

The first myth regarding the porn industry I'd like to address deals with something that hits very close to home.

Myth Number One:
All men in porn have large...?

(beat)

...mustaches.

This is simply not true. During my heyday in the Chico, California porn circuit of the late-1970s, I was well known (and admired) for my subtle Fu Man Chu.

Myth Number Two:
The porn industry is a veritable breeding ground for AIDS.
Once again, simply not true. Case in point. In my last feature

length film, *Skip Ching Does Iran*, I and my female counterpart were in the middle of a highly dramatic sexual scene when all of a sudden I said, 'Whoa! Cut. Stop rolling!' The reason being, I was without protection. Of course the Director was pissed off because I broke up the, you know, flow. But just like everyone on the set, he knew. Skip Ching didn't get this far in the business without being a professional. I won't lie, in the good old days, I might have gone bareback. But times, they are a-changing. Now I know better.

Skip Ching's A-Number One Rule: Absolutely no penetration shots without...?

That's right!

...Lubricant.

Believe me, I know.
There is nothing 'safe' about a heat rash.

Myth Number Three:
All dialogue in pornographic films is either...?

a) ad-libbed.
b) written on cue-cards.
c) not at all important.

Of course, the correct answer is...

d) pretty damn memorized!

Myth Number Four:
Contrary to the general female population, Oriental women
tend to have smaller...?

(beat)

...feet.

Again, untrue. Believe me. In my career as a leading man
of nearly three decades, there must have been over one
thousand and one different body parts in this here mouth.

Myth Number Five:
Upon leaving the fairly lucrative sex industry, many former
pornographic stars do not quite know what to do with the
remainder of their lives, spoiled as they have been, and thus
as a result begin to suffer from...depression.

(sigh)

Myth Number Six:
Pornography is not an Art.

Now here's one that hits particularly close to home.
You may be familiar with one of my most popular films from
the mid-'80s entitled, *Skip Ching and the Inflatable Woman*.
For which I might add I was nominated Best Supporting Actor

at the Golden Gland Awards in Punta Gorda, FL. Numerous people have stopped me on the street over the years and told me this particular film changed their perceptions about love and life and reality. In the movie, I portray a Plumber named... Skip Ching. One afternoon I make a service call to a beautiful woman's house. The woman happens to be Inflatable, and through the magic of movie-making, we proceed to get it on. But, over the course of the weeks that follow, something happens, and I begin to fall in love with this Inflatable Woman. So much so, that one night, delirious with envy, I break into her home and kill her husband and all her children by secretly deflating them.

Myth Number Seven:

Since the advent of the internet, Pornography has become the fastest growing form of media entertainment in the world. In America, Gay and Teen Pornography generates more income than Christian Rock and World Music combined. In a recent poll, six out of ten children under the age of fifteen have visited a pornographic website in the last month, and three out of ten consider themselves addicted to sexual voyeurism. In the pornographic industry, films in which Asian women are paired with one or more white men are considered Mainstream. Eleven independent pornographic videos last year starred a Black woman serving her Caucasian master, and six best-sellers in the last two years starred a Latina or Filipina playing the gartered role of housemaid, nanny, or live-in nurse to an invalid.

Videos portraying women raped and/or mutilated have tripled

each decade in North America since 1970. Others featuring
boys or girls under the age of twelve engaging in sex
acts with adults comprise currently the fastest growing
underground pornography market in the world.

And the…

Final Myth:

Fantasy leather-hoods Reality.

the man from guangdong

Before hosing down the fluorescent-flickering dish
room and kitchen floors and half-dozen grease grills at Johnny
Wong's Chinese Buffet, the man from Guangdong and I sit out
back on overturned five-gallon tofu buckets, trading silences. It
is an unusually cool night for mid-summer in Pueblo, Colorado.
The Taiwanese management and Mexican cook's gone home.
All the broken dishes swept into piles, the small metal dressing
cups and silverware hand-dug out of the garbage.

Marlboros and Vantages crackle minutely between
our lips.

Like this, he tells me of his tiny village on the southern
coast of China. How on some rare evenings just as the sun
is setting, a bright green haze radiates from a crack in the
ocean's horizon. A meteorological phenomenon. How in
summer when this happens, superstition claims you'll pull in a
good haul of crab and seabass the next morning. The evening
he snuck out of his country in a rusty hull, he thought he heard
the fishermen up on deck celebrating the mysterious light.
Then again, he may have only dreamt it.

The next ship the smugglers stowed him away in was
a freighter for a month.

We've been working together for two-and-a-half
months in the tiny kitchen at Johnny Wong's on the north side
of Pueblo, located on an otherwise dark block across the street
from a Popeye's Chicken and corner Amoco the neighborhood
kids call Murder Station. I drop heaping black bus tubs full of
greasy plates before him in the dish room, catch my breath
and watch his spray gun, blasting the fake china like Godzilla's
fire-breath in black-and-white movies.

Or, more often, he just waits in the corner by the stacked glass ashtrays, wiping sweat from his eyes with a sinewy forearm, half-listening to the FM classic rock station that was probably set a decade ago and never gets turned completely off.

I've left home a few months before, just barely graduating from high school. Packed my half-smashed soup can on wheels and headed in the opposite direction of everything I know because there is no one around me I want to be in the years to come. Not the success story of Henry Ford my Korean father once cut out from *Life Magazine* and taped to his bedroom mirror—a pale, brittled article of faith to lift him up and out of his auto mechanic pit. Not Mr. Choi who teaches tae kwon do and once a year at a sparsely filled Civic Auditorium allows a three-wheeler to pass over a bed of nails he's lying under. And definitely not my older brother returned from the Gulf, who thinks his veins are contaminated, and plays keno and blackjack every night at the Indian casino.

I'm seventeen and driving as fast as I can because soon it will be late autumn, and then winter with its blue evening crush and gravitational pull toward warm fear and comfort, and I can't end up selling water filters like my best friend Flick, or climb telephone poles and repair lines clumped with burnt flesh and feathers, or air conditioners, or miles of highway roads like Jonz, or, maybe, in a few short years, tend a sticky bar downtown and distribute pull tabs to factory workers who cough Plexiglas mucus into bare palms.

Quiet Asian kid scrawling rhymes on the insides of matchbooks. I may be ignorant, but my heart is a bat caught in broad daylight, so I follow it out of there. I leave, gas up, head South, then West. I'm not exactly sure. Anywhere out of the Midwest. My aunt in El Cerrito, the crazy one who married a white truck driver, says she'll take me in. Hook me up in her store selling beepers. My other option an Alaskan cannery. Maybe I'll find what I'm looking for in the eyes of a million fish.

The man from Guangdong laughs and tells me how he and the seventy other men and dozen women had to lie foot to cheek in the ship's hold for four weeks. No one had more than a pair of pants, two shirts, a pair of flip-flops. One rocky night someone pissed on his leg instead of in a tin can. For another two weeks he dreamed on and off of dragons swimming through blood and old leaves and sometimes the world up above was on fire.

America wasn't a place he ever thought he'd visit, let alone dream of leaving. He wanted to fish, or work in the shoe factory in the capital, like his father and uncles. But he was the oldest son. And then the Communists shut the factory down. No pensions. No nothing. So his family pooled all their savings and borrowed and begged and paid twenty grand to the illegal snakeheads who promised to smuggle him out. Nine thousand miles, from Guangdong Province, across the sea to Guatemala, up through Mexico, then Houston, L.A. The FBI busted a man he'd befriended on the three-month journey, and deported him. Two other men he knew died. Suffocated between cola and avocados in the back of a refrigerated semi just outside Dallas.

He wonders how long his luck will hold out. The owner of Johnny Wong's is a distant cousin, and pays him $3.80 an hour under the table. Of this cash, he wires 2/5 back to his village, and lives on the rest. Sometimes he listens to English conversation tapes on his only possession, a Walkman, while he runs the dishwasher, sounding out the hellos and how-are-yous with his thick purple lips, half dead from smoking so much. I don't always understand what he says, but his hands are articulate, nimble. I watch them, scarred by a lifetime of fishing line and hooks and saw-like teeth marks.

The Taiwanese Chinese in the kitchen don't speak his dialect. He's nothing to them anyway. A ghostly throwback to the Third World. One night they ask me to go drinking, someone has an old ID. They don't ask him. I follow and end up with a couple of others in a massage parlor at 4 a.m., throwing up beside a toilet with fuckheads pounding the door into a bruisy-hued dawn.

The next night, we close the restaurant alone, the man from Guangdong and I. I've rented a $75-per-week motel room on the edge of town, sick of stuffing myself into a sleeping bag at the rear of my fold-down hatchback. He lives in a boarding house owned by Johnny Wong on the opposite end of town. It's a particularly cold September night. The wind like barrels of ice water thrown in your face. He must be freezing in his ripped tee shirt so I ask him in the parking lot after close if he needs a ride home.

He declines, insists he doesn't like anything smaller than a bus.

"We'll flip for it," I say.

It's not clear who's got the luck tonight.

He hasn't shaved for days and has been losing weight. I see him back there behind all the steam and stainless steel a hundred times a night, dumping tub after tub, and don't know what to feel. Terror. Pity. Shame.

On the drive to his place, he asks me if I know of any other ways to make money.

"You think I'd be here if I did?" I say. It only feels partly true.

In the same measured voice he always uses, he tells me the snakeheads are now charging double. It's finally clear almost half of the men in his group didn't make it through, and the ones like him have to cover the loss. There's nothing he can do. They'll sever ears and lips, noses and eyes from his family if he doesn't start wiring the snakeheads $130 more a week.

I ask him what he's gonna do.

He shrugs and says that's the way the world works.

A cop turns on his cherries behind us.

He freezes, puts his hand on the door handle at forty miles per hour.

The cop passes, accelerates into the night.

We laugh, and he tells me he's so afraid here. He can't even buy liquor without an ID. He pays the other waiters to get him cartons of cigarettes because, though he's thirty-three years old, all the pimply convenience store attendants between home and work card him.

Around the corner from his boarding house, I stop and pick up a six-pack and bottle of Jack with my new fake ID that looks more like Jackie Chan than me.

In long stretches of silence, the man from Guangdong and I drink Mickeys on his cold front steps. The trees that aren't dead all look anemic. He tells me one day he'd like to marry a strong Chinese woman. Not an Americanized or city girl, who will cry when she's sad. But a woman with oceanic lungs who can blow life into the spirit he's lost.

A cop shines a spotlight on us, then passes.

He asks me what kind of girl I'm looking for. And I want to say—someone with an old soul, to hold in place my flimsy own. Someone whose eyes can cure. Instead, I tell him: someone pretty with nice skin, who'll sometimes ask me what I'm thinking.

He tells me there was a young woman in one of the freighters with him. A new soul who smelled of the pine needles she kept in her pocket for good luck. They spoke the same dialect and spent three weeks side by side, confined with the two dozen other Southern Chinese in the rusty hold of the ship, twenty-four hours a day, except once a week to bathe in icy sea water up on deck. To pass time on their backs in the dark, they talked about what they'd do in America; the businesses they'd each open. She was destined for Flushing, where she had a great aunt. He himself hadn't thought much further than to work as a farmer or kitchen hand to pay off the debt of his passage.

One night a snakehead, slurring Cambodian speech, came down into the hold. Clinking a rifle against the pipes. A former Khmer Rouge assassin turned people-smuggler. She went up with the man on deck without a fight. When she came back a few hours later, the girl didn't speak. For three days. And then, in darkness, she crawled to an opposite corner of the hold, over bodies too sick and tired to groan. And a couple of days later, the same clinking came back.

"Life no good for some," he says.

And I imagine my mother and father, the first time they must have kissed. Two war refugees, starving for love. And I see the man wishes he would have said something, to make the woman less numb. Even if only in the form of his hand, possessing nothing in the universe but warmth. But maybe even that would have been too much for her.

　　We pass the bottle and I ask if he could do anything with his life, what would it be. He smiles and takes a long drag and tells me how he's always wanted to work in an aviary. His great-grandfather maintenanced a large building, raising passenger pigeons in Guangdong. Gone now. Once, I tell him, I saw a movie on late night TV. *The Birdman of Alcatraz*. A true story about a slow-witted murderer in prison who stabs a guard when he's not allowed to see his visiting mother. He ends up sentenced to life in isolation. There he finds a wounded sparrow, nurses it back to health, and even teaches it to perform tricks. Over the decades, he becomes an expert on caged birds and even writes a book on the preventable diseases that kill them. One day he's visited by a woman, and together they start a business manufacturing medicine for birds.

　　When laughing, he sounds like my mother. A mutilated sing-song voice full of anticipation. Or are those tears behind his vocal chords? I can't tell, any more than I could with her. In more somber moments, the distant glaze in this foreigner's eyes is my older brother's when he used to take me fishing as a boy, watching the river for hours without talking. His anger and frustration when too many dirty dishes get dumped on him at once is the stifle my father swallowed each time he was passed up for a raise because of his accent. His cheeks, though, are mine, this man's from Guangdong. Sallow, and sunken behind all the steam, grease, and fluorescent shadows.

He keeps a dog from the city pound chained behind his boarding house. A scrawny, mean mongrel that claws at the dirt and beer cans, and whimpers at night. Neighborhood kids taunt the animal. Not black, not white, a sickly brown, yellowish around the pink eyes and gray jowls. I want to tell them the dog is the future state of their souls. To treat it well. Respectful that it has survived this long alone.

But I'm only a few years older than the hooded thugs who spit at the animal when it barks on its chain. A wild, angry thing. I'm American, and I don't have half the language this man from Guangdong possesses as he bolts out the back door wielding a cleaver.

The kids laugh and run.

Yell chingchongchinaman!

The dog whimpers.

The man is breathing hard.

A few sparse clouds oversee all.

And I know. In a thousand years, nothing will change.

We eat. We die. We search. Try to love in the dark.

The dog's soul isn't theirs, but mine. Look how he licks my hand when I come around. Limping after the old tennis ball I throw down the alley when we walk him. How he drops the round object in my palm, and bows. And I remember as a kid waking up in the middle of many nights beside my bed with the light still on. Hands clasped hard together. A dazed angel on the carpet fallen asleep mid-flight. A crooked crucifix on the wall, my only navigational device.

On my last night in Pueblo, Colorado, we go celebrate. He's wearing a new flannel shirt from the Salvation Army I showed him a week before. Scuffed hiking boots.

Getting ready for winter. He tells me he'll eventually try his luck in New Jersey, where a friend of a second cousin has a garage he can maybe live in. The bartender ignores us. Old White men with tattered sports caps and suspenders stare. So we buy a twelve of Modelo, go get the dog and walk down by the train tracks so the animal can run free.

He doesn't ask where I'm going, which of the red-markered lines on my soft-folded *Rand McNally Map of North America* I'll follow this time. Instead, he folds a boat from the brown paper bag and hands it to me along with a carton of Marlboros and a new jack-knife with the ideogram for *polestar* scraped on the blade. Both of which, I'll come to realize on the roads to follow, could feed a body in China for a whole week.

The blue evening winnows into a blood-singed horizon.
We don't speak.

IV.

vandalizing dreams

Three a.m. I stumble downtown to our favorite club, now a strip
    bar kitty-corner from Sex
World, to definitively refuse to ever dance with your memory
    again, and end up giving it a

pedicure. Or is this that library branch where we checked out
    poetry tapes to perform nightly
surgery on our dreams? No, now I remember, this dark
    building I'm pissing against

was a bakery where we broke the window and wounded the
    dough all night with our love so
the world could taste how much we wanted each other. I can still
    feel old layers of skin

laughing at the worst of your jokes. Like this one: a fool meets
    a princess dressed in armor
and steals her mule. No. What? A knight dresses as a princess
    to woo a horse. Whatever.

Back then I still believed resurrection was as inevitable as
    gasoline, a Fanta bottle and a lit
match around a U.S. military base in South Korea. You
    remember. Before hip-hop, the lull, a

longing to wander through a city vandalized by angels.
    Before your stilettoed lapdance across
my heart there were undertaker clothes stuffed in my ears. No.
    I considered myself an

architect of emotion and you were my little construction worker.
No, now I remember. You
were the mastermind and I was just the guy who delivered
flowers. It's coming back. A

gypsy drawing souls for a buck each set up his easel across
the street from our apartment on
Lyndale. I corrected that he couldn't possibly know truth, not
with that ridiculous tattoo of

God on his face, and the next day you bought a one-way ticket
to Luxembourg where you
claimed your destiny awaited. We argued all night over
adequate analogies for Soul to Spirit:

beef to apples, Louvre to MoMA, Mary Magdalene to Mary Had
a Little Lamb, ocean to
orgasm, parakeet to record player, old to new. At the airport I
asked you for an address, just

in case, and took every shortcut in the world to end up here. Yes.

riot in heaven *for Edward Song Lee (b. 1974 - d. 1992 in the L.A. Riots)*

there is only one corner grocery in heaven.
it is gigantic, the size of a million Wal-Marts.
here, you can find anything on the shelves.
prehistoric flint, pomegranates, magic carpets.
the only problem is the store is so large
you rarely see anybody else.
and however many things you can fit in your arms
you'll never find the checkout counter.
at first all my fingers were weighed down
by diamond and platinum rings.
now i only wear white-and-black jogging sweats and Adidas,
the old school kinds my parents bought me
when first we arrived in America.
sometimes while wandering these aisles
i stumble over piles of merchandise abandoned.
Barbie dolls, Van Gogh originals, sacks of spilled rice.
i pick the items up and put them back on their proper shelves
like i did all through my childhood in Koreatown.
only now i don't mind it so much.

when i arrived, some of the rioters
who didn't know they were dead
roved up and down these rows pushing
shopping carts loaded with stereos and VCRs,
huffing crazed looks on blood-streaked faces,
their lopsided bodies shadowless under fluorescence.
the original Tyndale Bible i once found
trampled in the Meat section. its pages
scattered with bootprints.
                              i unpeeled them
and put the book back with the others
in Sacred Texts.

　　　　　　　as i passed i saw the Devil
folded in dark contemplation.
then again, it may have been Jesus
wrapped in smoldering saffron.
or some Buddhist monk;
i've followed a few of them around...

once, i spotted Latasha Harlins:
that black girl from South Central who punched
a Korean shopkeeper in the face
a year before the fires
over accusations and a bottle of orange juice
then got shot in the back walking out...

she was standing in a Raiders jersey
on the far end of Music & Entertainment.

　　　　　　Latasha! i called out.
i was moving fast, because around here
you only get one chance if you recognize someone.
　　　　　　Latasha!
she looked up from a CD case and i saw her eyes widen.
　　　　　　Wait, don't run!
then she turned around and pulled out a gun.
i could hear her headphones still blaring.
Don't come any closer! she yelled.
　　　　　　The Korean lady who shot you! i said. She went insane!
Step back yo or I'll blow your head off!!
　　　　　　My mother sang with her in church choir!
I said stay the fuck back!!!
　　　　　　But it's all right now!

71

Are you fucking deaf you dumb—!!!

[GUN EXPLODES]

    of course,
even in heaven you can't die twice.
so i just stood there, my heart
dripping through my fingers
like wealth in my father's unfortunate line.

maybe i should have chased after her;
tried to explain desperation
knows no race,
no color, no culture…

but it was too late,
again.

next time.

the invisible church

A park in a country.
But which country?

If you ask the Somali men hovering
over ancient chessboard tables
and apple tea where they are,
they'll tell you a constant state of waiting.
And that all the broken glass on the sidewalk
reminds how dangerous it is to pray on their knees
in Arabic these days.

The Hmong man with military medals and a gray goatee
bears a different story. He plays it on his kher,
a two-string spidery bamboo violin he leans into,
slicing open one ghost at a time with his bow.
If he set out a hat, or tin can, maybe
all the shoes hating dead leaves
wouldn't sound so lonely.

A war and a Tuesday afternoon.

But which war? If you stop
the glaucomic Polish Jew who hobbles
past crackheads on picnic tables feeling their bones,
or young du-rags dreaming new tags,
that punctual spirit, he might tell you
he escaped from a concentration camp by hand-washing yellow stains
from SS pillow cases and bed sheets; propelled
to safety through a laundry chute and survived
the winter forest on roots and worms...

Or, this autumn, he might just say the crude
tattoo numbered on the inside of his wrist
is a postage stamp on a strange envelope
lost in transit.

Actually, he's probably heading to the thrift store
to see if any stained-glass lamps, board games,
or good cutlery came in.

A country and a soul.

Among a hip-hop boom box and Russian card game on a
        one-board bench;
an old drunk Mexicano in straw cowboy hat and white beard,
belting a cappella harvest hymns of a woman with bad intentions
and the scrawny mutt who pants in front of me,
leash in mouth...

There is a small city park and fountain
presided over by the Saint of Looted Expression.
Some days after work I'll breach the dry basin
and sit at the statue's bare feet. Read
a news page to assess the world's ever-fading progress.
I'll go until my eyes, the ink and evening
blend to a volatile cocktail. Or
a jittery spirit approaches from nowhere
to ask in secret code for the church that burned down
long before either of us was born.

seasons of hair

I know men who survive
by their women's hair, its scent
a force field each winter dawn
shuffling steps at the bustop

In spring, smiles resurface, hands
hungry to unjam storm windows,
re-thread bolts and grease bicycle chains;
clanks under engine blocks
drive wasps crazy; a dancing
ankle turned on a wine bottle in the grass

Summer evenings around a picnic
table metropolis'd with food and condiments
the man's fingers sweep the moon
from his wife's black mane, humming
of lovers in an oarless boat on the East Sea...
while breezes blanket our exhaustion
from an afternoon full of trees

But my favorite season is autumn,
when my father's evening tea changes color
for all the leaves fallen into the river,
and my mother rests on the sofa
after work and asks
me to remove any silver
from her hair
like sewing in reverse

ID #452-7B9

i never dreamed in America
everything would be so large.
feet. hands. my friend in Saigon,

Lan Do, pulled my tee shirt from the factory
bus into a crowded office where they took
our measurements and photographs in a tight blouse

then asked of our favorite American foods.
i said creamy noodles. the office clerk looked
up at me over fashionable glasses.

so i said hamburgers.
no one has chosen my friend yet
because she is not as pretty a girl

as me. her picture from six years ago
still appears on the internet.
sometimes my finger rests the cursor

over her shiny face, mature
for her age, its nub of a nose,
across the sunken eyes,

always too sleepy and small.
her forehead is nice though;
round, it gathers light well

like heaven's kiss. she will
make a good wife; contemplative,
unlike me who likes to eat

cheese puffs and watch cable TV all night
while my American husband snores
like a cat dreaming of soft edible grass.

sometimes at the computer
i run the cursor over her throat,
Lan Do, and click ten or twenty times—fast,

until the desk lamp ticks
a degree dimmer or the screen
freezes and i go to bed.

once during the monsoon season
Lan Do and i sat on the damp earth
of her aunt's shanty and compared

our bodies, palm to palm,
sole to filthy foot, without releasing
even our eyes from one another's

hold; we pretzeled our skinny selves
and giggled until the neighbor's goat
wandered in. other children

soon followed, singing to the beat
of galvanized zinc. Lan Do's teeth
were missing in front. mine have

always gleamed the brightest.
my fingers and toes measured longer
that afternoon rain relieved the swelter,

and would only grow more
over the months to follow.
i don't know why. we ate

the same rice stick and mint leaves,
a daily rambutan, sweet to lick its milky
underskin. they say it is in one's genes, but

we were both raised by distant relatives,
two in a gray river of war infants,
so there is no way to learn the truth.

the first night my husband
pushed himself into my bottom,
my eyes began to tear.

spirit and blood,
like water to a starving anemic.
now he warns me each time with a kiss

on the small of my back, moist
and tender, to root
my fear of falling forever.

from my allowance to shop
for groceries and maternity wear
in the afternoons, i am saving

each week a little more.
one day when i have enough
i will rest the computer's cursor

on Lan Do's forehead,
place my order
and disappear.

kabuki kong's final song

last week i had a match against a brand new guy
brought down from Montreal. Kid Canuck,
they call him. long blonde hair, tan, all bulked up
in white trunks with a red maple leaf,
you know where. some rich producer's nephew.
he was scheduled to wrestle The Sheik in the night's third match,
but the old guy had a hernia while they was warming up
so the producer put me on the bill against Kid Canuck
at the last minute. we didn't have time to choreograph much
action.
the guy was cocky. and green. three minutes in,
here comes his hand up in my hair, yanking away, hard, for real!
dragging me on my ass around the ring,
he wasn't telegraphing his headbutts neither.
soon enough my nose was a cherry caught under a dumptruck.
the blood all over sure got the crowd into it, boy.
up till then, they was kinda quiet, waiting for the federation
champion
the Texas Tornado to take on the Human Jackhammer.
i told him to ease up, but the Kid was so jacked up by now
he couldn't hear nothing. dancing around, slapping
all the white kabuki powder off my face. raking my eyes. tearing
my black kimono
between his teeth. cursing at me in bad French.
not even bothering to pretend my karate chops was hurting him!

now, i can take just about anything. ask anyone.
over the years, i've been pile-drived, clothes-lined, and suplexed
into losses by the best of them.
but on this particular night, something happened to
Kabuki Kong,

and one pop i took in the chops
shot my adrenaline way up,
my blood flowing all over hell now
like carbolic acid, and him twisting my arm for real!
not giving a flying fuck about my bad elbow,
my bad back,
my bad marriage,
or my eight-year-old son Duane
who don't even like to watch his daddy wrestle no more,
'cause he's ashamed, 'cause deep down
he don't know what to believe in,
and the next thing i knew i had the pretty-boy sonofabitch
Kid Canuck down hard on the mat in a scorpion leg-lock!!!

the referee didn't have no choice but to throw
my arm up under the lights.
i was a little dazed yet as they hauled Kid Canuck off
on a stretcher.
the audience didn't know quite what to think about that.
half of them was already wearing the free Kid Canuck tee shirts
the promoters handed out for coming early.

but then, slowly, someone in the far corner of the arena
started making some noise.
and soon more people started in.
it was a chemical thing. some people
in the upper bleachers stood up,
then all of them were, everywhere! yelling
and cheering! and not 'cause they hated
the other guy, they didn't!
they was cheering 'cause i beat the guy

fair and square! and they knew it! he gave up!
right there in the middle of the ring, out of pain!
i had him down in that scorpion leg-lock a good two minutes,
screaming like a baby, like a cut pig, like a man in real pain,
and they knew it! you can't fake that!
they'd seen so much phony bullshit through the years,
and they could tell...

this match was different.

and they appreciated that.
they appreciated being shown the truth just once
in their sorry-ass lives...

even if it was proved to them by a man in white makeup,
with a black kimono on, named
Kabuki Kong,
who just by looking at him,
no one would ever believe
underneath is a true
American Champion.

waiting on the other side

I.

Hours after it's ripped Red Lake County a new orifice, you mute
the news in bed and muse of the tornado's soul. My half-dream
a ghostly eon away. *Maybe*, you say. *There's a child
buried alive. Its vocal chords too loose now.*

The condom still on me, a melted elf back-lit by the wreckage
of a gutted school and post office beaming at us from the TV,
339 miles away, north past Anoka, amidst dairy farms
we'll drive along the next morning; pole barns and water towers
like little boys fantasizing themselves giant robots.
Autumn leaves whirling mid-highway their crazy Sufi jigs...

II.

Isn't this how you settled in me in the first place?
Piecemeal, disastrous—in long, disturbing blinks; frustrated rabbit
jabs; a rain of flowers and oil paints.
I remember one night falling in love with your hair
as if a separate person like your two-second mealtime prayers.
In a song your plastic brush mended all summer,
I could almost taste every wound I'd ever bandaged
by smearing hurt against the world. All the promises
lost underwater a day before winter.

III.

Every downed mile marker is a kind of relinquishment.
Every car and minivan overturned in a field fetused with beets.
The carapace of a plastic swimming pool
highballed mid-road with hail and brown sluice. To the west
the smoking lobotomy of a grain elevator and hog farm
myriad-haloed by black flies; each standing
evergreen more lovely-littered than the last…

And suddenly I could hear again our flimsy door
on Minnehaha Avenue—a drunken wind
trumpeting off-key all that autumn you got word
a car bomb caught your brother in Afghanistan; the handwriting
in his last letter submerged in pure white-hot anger
at you for your anti-war protest and exhibit. And then
the bitter calls from your father and sisters…

The only X-mas gift sent that year the lace
of frost accumulated on our door mat,
which meant despite everything and anyone at least
the stars had all cast their ballots in favor of us!
Or so I tried to convince…
All your drawing pads steam-
pressed on the radiator by then…

IV.

Yes. This is how I'll see you always: at twelve mph
trolling a buckled highway shoulder match-sticked

with telephone poles, sod, glistening roadkill...
A legion of cops and emergency workers waving batons
and glo-sticks in blue evening for us to *Slow Down!*
These public servants in hats and rain slickers,
the most functional guardians of heaven or hell imaginable.
We'll get through, you whisper, touching my thigh.
That's where all the answers are.

airport matchmaker

She believes, this half-blind Korean halmoni,
in miraculous sunderings. See the perfect lyrics
magpies sing to broken pumpkins on her quivering lips.
This old face reader, who's waved me over.

Is it the white Reeboks on her feet like mushrooms
my mother collected on a summer hill
that make me finally sit? Or her offer
to prognosticate my future?

However anonymous, the sun loves each crevice
of her face. Decades freckled, she is an autumn rice field
before machines dappled the land. I listen
to the bodies buried in her half-chant
of the importance of family.

With gravity, she stares and warns I must wed
a Korean woman. One whose forehead is round
enough to translate the moon's wishes; whose strength
roots the universe in the blackness of our hair.
Generous lips, she advises, will flavor any emptiness,
and there will be many such evenings. Primal things,
like listening to someone's skin. A woman whose loss
when first we kiss equals the weight of my belonging...

How to enter the past as she returns to it
so quietly, earth-struck, just outside of Atlanta?

The years, she says, taking my palm,
press our beings like moist shadows, nourishing
what our actions, in sum, fail to see,

leaving us in certain moments dry
on the other side of life, a strange witness
to all we believe. Like leaves playing
tag in an abandoned courtyard.
Footsteps through mud
that realize they will never arrive...

My airplane is boarding first, but her tiny grip only tightens.

The pleasantries over, now her nostalgia speaks
of the rhythm of cool nights and solitary knitting;
how together they comprise a warmth
one can wear like a sad smile or silver hairpin
plunged deep in the soil during a war...

To feed the future.

how they linger

To the fetus, the girl's menthol cigarette
must have crackled like jet-exploded

debris over the city. Neither had ever seen
the shaded building, more family split-level

than clinic. His words
like geese, too far to hone

in on the heart she kept
trying to swallow. Degrees

cooler now than the night
they first caressed on a city bus

gift-wrapped in time and light;
his wild, rubbery vocabulary

melted by her skin; the scent
of her hair—a spring forest asleep.

Here's a clue years later
they'll see one another across a tapas bar

and joke of jobs, sightings of schoolmates;
evasively shrugging, eyes awrinkle:

The girl is holding her own hand
in the Mazda he's borrowed from a friend.

Maybe to pray, if she's even sure
what to stare at in the parking lot

and wish. It doesn't matter. Now
he's asking if she's thirsty.

He's packed a cooler of fruit juice
and sandwiches. Flowers

decided against. Yet
the one thing

missing. Ancient, simple
heat: violets, a rose, daisies.

Nothing too awkward in color
or form to ever remind

of anything. But something
at least to preserve

how they linger.

real karaoke people

when you're singing karaoke
there are more important things than staying in tune;
more important than keeping the beat;
stretching the high notes to that sweet spot in the wind…

when you're singing karaoke,
really singing from the center of your being,
in whatever town you're in, whatever bar, club or smoky poolroom
you find your spit-bright rainbow sizzling
the one hot stage light on a Tuesday evening,
jukebox broken, stars
a million faceless frozen angels,

the only thing that really matters is…

                    Destiny

and how much you can affect it with the far end of your voice.
how much you can stand up to it,
eye to eye,
tooth to tooth;
try to change it,
then, finally, in the end
give up
and love it, that joke called
                                your Fate
with all its flaws…

like your voice
                                filling the void…

You never close your eyes
        anymore

        when I kiss your lips...

real karaoke people
don't make it to church very often.
or the gym. they don't play the trombone or violin,
they practice no art, no deception.
real karaoke people
don't even know what age they are,
or they would never get up there.
they don't know their class or race,
at least while they're singing...

the street's as hard and cold as it's gonna get,
so real karaoke people float, cuz they know
they can't fall through it...

And they sit at the bar
and put bread in my jar
and say: Man
        what are you doing here...!

real karaoke men
wear white underwear
and find strange comfort in cubicles.
they mess the damp heads of their children out of reflex
at eight o'clock, when they hang their suitcoats and hats on the rack

like scarecrows; compete with shadows;
make love to their wives of twenty-eight years
with only a magic sack of tricks, a purple pill,
and liniment. everything they eat lately
tastes like last week's chicken. they've quit
smoking, and now chew things,

        as the soul deep down
        chews things...

Now,
at the end of the road...

        Still I can't let you go...

there is nothing pretty about
real karaoke women. neck veins
engorged, mouths
wide open; cigarette-stained teeth and lips
puffing smoke signals for...
                Love
                      if you can cut it.

real karaoke women
pop buttons; plant roses
with the gravity of their focus;
raise the dead beloved
in the rise and fall of their voices.

real karaoke women
like my mother

have breath that reeks of night wind, myth, fugitive
streams trickling poems folded from lilies
just over the mountain...

ari ari rang
suri suri rang
ararii ka naan-nae...aeaeae
aaa-rirang   mm mm mm mm mm

  arari-ka-ah nan-nae.....

ten thousand years away,
in a mythical land called America,
I spill whiskey between friends in New York,
32nd and Broadway, where a big screen TV and karaoke
machine can bliss your fix till six a.m.;
half-a-dozen private rooms, song books
by the twos and threes catch the stray flecks
of a silvery disco planet whirling overhead...

karaoke songs in Chinese, Japanese, Spanish, English, Korean,
    Indonesian, Vietnamese...

real karaoke people know
past three a.m., English
can be only half a home;

the rest you have to excavate with your throat;
a subtle archeology around land mines
and sun-bleached bones;

one hip-hop away
from a gunshot that wakes your dead grandfather;
one missed beat of crowded
wartime train doors
closing
between your refugee family.

real karaoke people,
like my aunt,
don't like to swim for sport;
the sharks' blood they see in their dreams
might make them think
they're still sinking,

so she sings…

Memories,
all alone in da moonlight.
> *I can smile*
> *at da old days,*

I was beau-ti-pul den…
> *I rememba*
> *da time I knew*
> *what heppiness waz…*

real karaoke people
> have bad memories.

that's why
they need
the words
            at the bottom of the screen.

Every song loves a new story.

thrown —*for A.M.*

Those were moments of stones, hand-packed clay,
firecrackers, stained glass, footballs and fists driven into
pimply faces calling you chink, gook, the fuck yous, and
everything else you threw, to be tough, fight back, to feel your
own rage, what flying was like in one sore arm, hurling a black
rubber ball at the side of a factory all summer, sliders through
rain, breaking bats and the skin on your knuckles against
sheetrock, plywood frames, stucco and cement, like another
boy in some lost age might have axed a path through the
forest, or eviscerated a cow—

                                    Balls turn to beer bottles, front
grilles and cracked windshields; three probation officers;
sipping Everclear all ninth grade in that back alley, that river
cave, that abandoned Northern Pacific boxcar, sizzling chronic
colds and nosebleeds off a white-hot mirror you smashed for
seven more years of what you thought couldn't possibly get
worse,

        running out the front door from a crazy man with a limp
and loaded twelve-gauge, your own father, who swore in a
language you could hardly remember, and so laughed at like
water on a grease fire; spat buckshot words back you knew he
couldn't understand, so hurt worse, like cocksucker! through
shivers, a steel barrel piercing your chest

                                    until one midnight
you packed a garbage bag, popped a downhill clutch and
bolted over highways and cornfields; bright-lit cities of alcohol,
mushroom and acid-infused blues; Kansas City in a fourteen-
dollar-a-night motel with that girl's wicked drawl that first

crackled through a KFC late-night drive-thru speaker; her
sweet skin to the dry bread of your own like warm butter;
Montreal, Juarez, tipping topless waitresses at the razor-wire
border of heaven, or was it hell?—

                Still throwing things out of car
windows: dead birds, stolen stereos, work bandages and
baggies licked clean to air all the moldy rooms you ever tried
to laugh at yourself in—propelled by some wind or power or
dream your mother had that you would make it to California,
Colorado, New York, and all the way back to that Minneapolis
ledge you stood on with your friend, Andrew, another lost,
brotherless Asian man with no face or voice in this land,
balancing mid-winter with a bottle of Wild Turkey in one hand,
reeling on that Gold Medal Flour factory rooftop overlooking
the Mississippi, slurring drunk debates all night over the war
in the Gulf, conspiracy theories, freak accidents, religion
and fate—

                like how on Lake Street one wet July, mosquito
dirges by starlight, a comet scraped high across the
atmosphere, and we remembered that astronaut lady from
the space shuttle Challenger who never got her Sally Ride
back—a draining cloud of smoke for a soul who wanted to fly,
like anyone, any earthling, but maybe it just wasn't her time—

Between throwing and flying, not everyone comes back.

I did. Andrew didn't. I should have heard the paranoia's
triumphant rattle in his throat; witnessed with my two clearer
eyes my best friend spiraling through blackness—a final

plummet no blunt, no high, no amount of smoke or needle
could store inside.

But life, even when falling, rubs and tears at the dark.

Years later, his seed of a son named Han, born in the
aftermath of his father's deserted life, just three weeks after
ashes shaped final wings over the northern shore of Lake
Michigan,

now plays Tchaikovsky on piano. This beautiful hoarse-
voiced boy with little hands so sticky they somehow stretch
to reach a far key just in time. Some days they don't make it,
or land wrong, but he doesn't stop. With the seriousness of
a miniscule saint tucked in his brow, he plays with the focus
and grace his father, before losing all, once argued with me in
defense of God—

           I want to tell him, this stubborn five-year-
old I watch while his mother works at the Chinese restaurant,
trying to be two parents, trying to feed him with art, common
sense and reverence for a Korean-Chinese-Vietnamese-
American story of the past no one will ever be able to translate
for him—

           I want to tell him not to listen when his older
fourth- and sixth-grade neighbors taunt, shouting fag! for
practicing Vivaldi or *Carmen* on a Saturday afternoon; sit back
down, more will come… But who am I to grasp at anyone
when all I could ever hold has flown, sputtered, exploded mid-
air like too much need crammed inside a prayer? Who am I to

demand when anyone dares try to silence him, when he dares silence himself, to keep stretching his hands over that sea of black-and-white keys, don't stop, keep pumping those brass pedals with your tiny feet, life isn't perfect, almost never adds up, and it sure the hell won't last, so fuck it, dig deep and just keep throwing yourself, something, anything for as long and hard and far as you can...

and I promise you,

I swear to God,

one day

it'll all come back.

acknowledgments

Many thanks to the editors at the following publications in which several of the poems in this collection, in part or full, have appeared: *Ache Magazine, Crab Orchard Review, The Journal of the Asian American Renaissance, KoreAm Journal, Korean Quarterly, Mizna, O.K.A.Y.*, and *Water~Stone Review*, as well as to the editors of *The Best Ten-Minute Plays 2004* and *Take Ten II,* in which "Kabuki Kong's Final Song" first appeared as part of a longer work.

Sincere gratitude also to the Millay Colony for the Arts, the Minnesota State Arts Board, the Loft Literary Center, SASE, the Blacklock Nature Sanctuary, and the Jerome Foundation for their generous support for work on these poems.

Finally, for their graciousness, deep appreciation to my family and David Mura, Bao Phi, Suzanne, Mindy, Sun Yung, Mali, Mike, Sarah, Alejandra, Julayne, Charissa, Andy, Paul, Wing, Rich, Sandra, Ann, Tatiana, Sherry, Carolyn, Ellen, Mark, Marie, Brooke, Kurt, Na-la-ri, Ken, Me-K, Walter, Chamindika, Diaspora Flow, Juliana, Annelize, Manny, Thuyet, POC Soccer, Heather, Mai Neng, Bryan, Ka, Reggie, Tou, Wei-li, Sandy, Jacob, Alice, Fong, Sophie, Deborah, Ishle, Kai, Tracey, Sheila, Alexs, Eric, Robert, David, Two Tongues, Isangmahal, APIA Summit spirits, Feedback, Undocumented Sons, the Asian American Writers' Workshop, AK Connection, Dalros Design, AAR, the Playwrights' Center, PCTV, Augsburg College, the Guthrie Theater, Ma-Yi Theater, MN Slam, Theater Mu, MNSWA, the New York Theatre Workshop, Intermedia Arts, the MN Advocates for Human Rights, the Native American Journalists Association, and everyone at New Rivers Press.

biography

photograph by
Charissa Uemura

ED-BOK LEE attended kindergarten in South Korea, and grew up in North Dakota and Minnesota. He's studied at the Universities of California-Berkeley, Minnesota, Kazakh State-Almaty, and Brown University, where he earned an MFA in Creative Writing. Among his awards are grants from the Minnesota State Arts Board, the Loft Literary Center, SASE, the Jerome Foundation, and the National Endowment for the Arts. Currently based in Minneapolis and New York, he regularly performs his poetry and writes for theaters across the country.